WATCHING A MAN BREAK A DOG'S BACK

# TOM WAYMAN

## Watching a Man Break a Dog's Back

*Poems for a Dark Time*

**HARBOUR
PUBLISHING**

HARBOUR PUBLISHING CO. LTD.
P.O. Box 219, Madeira Park, BC, VON 2H0
www.harbourpublishing.com

Edited by Silas White
Cover photograph by Luis Hidalgo
Cover design by Anna Comfort O'Keeffe
Text design by Shed Simas / Onça Design
Printed and bound in Canada
Printed on 100% recycled paper

Harbour Publishing acknowledges the support of the Canada Council for the Arts, the Government of Canada, and the Province of British Columbia through the BC Arts Council.

LIBRARY AND ARCHIVES CANADA CATALOGUING IN PUBLICATION
Title: Watching a man break a dog's back : poems for a dark time / Tom Wayman.
Names: Wayman, Tom, 1945- author.
Identifiers: Canadiana (print) 20190234164 | Canadiana (ebook) 20190234172 | ISBN 9781550179125 (softcover) | ISBN 9781550179132 (HTML)
Classification: LCC PS8595.A9 W38 2020 | DDC C811/.54—dc23

# OTHER BOOKS BY TOM WAYMAN

## Poetry

*Waiting for Wayman* (1973)

*For and Against the Moon* (1974)

*Money and Rain* (1975)

*Free Time* (1977)

*A Planet Mostly Sea* (1979)

*Living on the Ground* (1980)

*Introducing Tom Wayman: Selected Poems 1973–80* (1980)

*The Nobel Prize Acceptance Speech* (1981)

*Counting the Hours* (1983)

*The Face of Jack Munro* (1986)

*In a Small House on the Outskirts of Heaven* (1989)

*Did I Miss Anything? Selected Poems 1973–1993* (1993)

*The Astonishing Weight of the Dead* (1994)

*I'll Be Right Back: New & Selected Poems 1980–1996* (1997)

*The Colours of the Forest* (1999)

*My Father's Cup* (2002)

*High Speed Through Shoaling Water* (2007)

*Dirty Snow* (2012)

*Winter's Skin* (2013)

*The Order in Which We Do Things: The Poetry of Tom Wayman*
    (ed. Owen Percy; 2014)

*Built to Take It: Selected Poems 1996–2013* (2014)

*Helpless Angels* (2017)

# Fiction

*Boundary Country* (2007)
*A Vain Thing* (2007)
*Woodstock Rising* (2009)
*The Shadows We Mistake for Love* (2015)

# Non-fiction

*Inside Job: Essays on the New Work Writing* (1983)
*A Country Not Considered: Canada, Culture, Work* (1993)
*Songs Without Price: The Music of Poetry in a Discordant World* (2008)
*If You're Not Free at Work, Where Are You Free?: Literature and Social Change* (2018)

# Edited

*Beaton Abbot's Got the Contract: An Anthology of Working Poems* (1974)
*A Government Job at Last : An Anthology of Working Poems* (1976)
*Going for Coffee: Poetry on the Job* (1981; 1987)
*East of Main: An Anthology of Poems from East Vancouver* (co-edited with Calvin Wharton; 1989)
*Paperwork: Contemporary Poems from the Job* (1991)
*The Dominion of Love: An Anthology of Canadian Love Poems* (2001)

# CONTENTS

## O Calgary: The World Awry

## Jazz on a Rainy Afternoon: Elegies

## A Door in a Wood: Words

# ACKNOWLEDGEMENTS

Many thanks to the editors and staff of the following publications, in which poems of mine appeared (sometimes in earlier versions):

*The Almagre Review*: Jazz on a Rainy Afternoon; Tim Hardin Eats Breakfast

*The Antigonish Review*: Absence

*Arc Poetry Magazine*: Literally

*Canadian Literature*: In a Bleak Time; Wind Elegy

*Cloudbank*: Three Words

*COG*: The Interview; The Message

*The Dalhousie Review*: Meadow

*Forklift, Ohio*: Not the Wind

*FreeFall*: Carrying Patrick Lane; Time Seasons

*Grain*: Green Man, Raven; How I Achieved Tenure

*Hanging Loose*: Desolatia; A Meeting with Pete Seeger in a Starbucks in Kennewick, Washington During the 2016 Federal Election

*The Hudson Review*: The Stain

*Literary Review of Canada*: Release

*The Malahat Review*: The Air; Leaflets

*New Ohio Review*: My Life with Pines

*The New Orphic Review*: The Rage of the Snowplow

*The New Quarterly*: Bedspread

*Poet Lore*: Fifty Years of Stacking Chairs

*Poetry*: O Calgary

*Poetry East*: Why I Write

*Prairie Fire*: Rant: Lilacs

*Prism international*: The Door

*Queen's Quarterly*: Kim Kratky (1946-2013)

*Saranac Review*: Rant: Who I Write For
*subTerrain*: Maybe
*Windfall*: House Made of Mist


"Fifty Years of Stacking Chairs" was featured on *Poetry Daily* (poems.com) on April 30, 2017. "Literally" was awarded the 2017 Confederation Poets Prize for the best poem published in *Arc* in 2016.


In memory of Colleen Couves, Pier Giorgio Di Cicco, David Piasta and Alicia Priest.

# O CALGARY

*The World Awry*

*I live in a remote mountain valley of surpassing natural beauty in all four seasons. But the region where I make my home is not immune to the history it is living through. Similarly, I bring to the people, fields, roads, rivers and forests under these peaks my own history, personality and consequent responses to the locale and years I inhabit.*

*My poems absorb and set forth again this mix of concerns: my and my neighbours' attempts to build a life immersed in natural splendours, a dysfunctional body politic often crippled by unrestrained greed, fear and spitefulness, and a personal past and present that at my age leads me to take stock of what I think I know. I see the biosphere and the human community around me pummelled daily by the four hammers of the current economic order, with the blows of each of the four facilitating the pounding of the others. Two hammers are the ever-widening gap between the very rich and the rest of us, and the deindustrialization of the community as jobs are moved offshore and the nation increasingly reverts to our former colonial status: supplier of raw materials, and purchaser of goods and services manufactured elsewhere. The other two hammers are the permanent personal debt offered to the citizenry as the means to keep an economy functional without enough adequate jobs, and the steady participation of the nation's military in civil wars overseas: Afghanistan, Libya, Iraq, Syria.*

*Like most people my age, I can remember when the continual blows from these hammers did not distort and defile individuals, communities and the nation. One consequence of how society is organized at present is a surging lack of empathy—hence this book's title. Adding to the shared degradation of our era are efforts to prevent a unified rejection by the population of the current societal arrangements. Group is pitted against group, with the resultant divisiveness engineered and abetted by the well-paid and the well-meaning alike. Cherry-picking of historical tragedies and attempts to shame this or that segment of the country's inhabitants are among the arsenal of approaches aimed at separating Canadians from each other.*

*The poems of this section take our present predicament as their theme. The poem addressed to Calgary intends to refer to a set of beliefs and behaviours popularly ascribed—especially in the part of the world where I live—to Calgarians. These abhorred values and actions are emblematic of the personal and social distortions arising from the pursuit of wealth above every other concern. The poem doesn't mean to impugn the actual city of Calgary, which contains the usual mix of people and attitudes, any more than an invocation of Jerusalem in a religious context is intended to describe the real city's manifold residents, social structures, faiths, etc.*

# Restoration of Order

As the club connects,
a sheet of pain and rage, or of agony
and fear, spurts inward. The uniformed arm
holding the weapon
descends again: an elbow raised
to protect its body
fractures, a chip of bone from a skull
is driven into the membrane intended to protect the brain,
and as the stick hits the side of a face
the concussion splits an eardrum.

The officially issued club
repeatedly smashes downwards
amid an oceanic roar of terror, confusion,
protest—the animal cry
of revolt, heard in the streets
since there *were* streets. Always those sleeves
with their insignia are hoisted and fall
as though fists that clutch sledge handles
are pounding a barrier into place
to contain a flood. Screams and shouts
which the thudding of the clubs punctuate
can, however, only briefly be subdued
into the silence of an abandoned, littered
avenue. The following night,
a week from now, a decade after today,

the water of rebellion will seep
under or around
the continually rebuilt embankment.

This recurring storm
of thousands of sign-bearers chanting,
of a downpour of rocks, nerve gas projectiles, flaming bottles,
beatings at emergency aid stations, bullets,
a designated area for
the temporary morgue
constitutes weather authority would outlaw
if it could. Yet wherever the restoration of order
is proclaimed, other words are audible
despite the curfew, the government's casualty figures,
or the absence of any news report at all
about what happened here. Water when obstructed
pushes below ground
to emerge in mall parking lots,
the basements of banks and office towers,
and appears through sidewalk cracks
in front of factories and transit stops.
When this fluid touches air, a cacophony rings out:
of suppressed accusations, votes
at banned meetings, testimony from
the ignored. If the streets that might otherwise hear
are empty except for security patrols,
or are indifferent, or discouraged,
the sound becomes absorbed by
the DNA of sycamore and oak that line boulevards,

of cottonwood windbreaks alongside fields,
and of mountainside fir and spruce.
On the molecules of water vapour
that float free from these trees
into jails and executive suites alike
is inscribed the future.

# Leaflets

*It's the minutes' war.*
—Tomas Tranströmer, "Leaflet"
(trans. John F. Deane)

How many of these slips
passed from my fingers
into the fingers of the dubious
the mildly curious, the automatically polite
the supporters, the ones who thought I spoke too quickly
who wanted time to consider
what they believed I was saying

Grape boycott, lettuce boycott
Why the war was wrong
At a protest, the reasons a slogan or stance was correct
compared to other slogans or positions
A warning against *agents provocateurs*
The arguments in favour of a strike
The reasons this picket line should be honoured
Why a union continues to be the only way
to defend against the arbitrary meanness of management
The facts that made the cut in welfare rates a scandal
The past actions of an official about to give an address
which needed to be opposed

To show how the Earth cannot be saved
without social control of industry

Hands swollen and calloused with labour
received these printed sheets, also hands with many rings
and hands with nails painted in the latest shade
because a job depended on dressing as fashionably as possible
on a meagre salary
Hands blank as the faces that
looked down at the leaflets received them
Angry hands that crumpled the paper
and threw it onto the sidewalk in front of me

—as many and diverse hands
as minutes in an hour, a lifetime
as trees that stand on the mountains
that surround the valley, the city
—some of these fir and pine
destined themselves to become leaflets
but that for now remain patient
enduring, oblivious

# Fifty Years of Stacking Chairs

I fold two and carry one in each hand
between the small groups of people still talking
although most have left the room. I lean the chairs
on ones already upright against a wall
or lower them atop a horizontal pile.

Two of these chairs at a time
are easily manageable, so back at the empty rows
I fold three and haul them with both hands
across the space. Next trip I try
four: fingers on each hand curved
under the metal backrests of
two chairs. Fifty years

of unstacking and arranging them: centre aisle
or not? Straight lines or semicircle?
Then clearing them. Anti-war event,
community protest meeting, union meeting,
address by a notable or activist figure
in a cause I endorse, or by a novice
or veteran writer, or panel involving
three speakers. Fractious debates, or
readings or talks I can hardly stay awake through
—chair after chair after chair:
my twenties, forties, seventies. Other volunteers,

fellow members, friends of friends helping,
and now the tables used by the presenters

at the front, or to collect tickets at the door,
must be tilted on one edge, the slide that locks the legs
released, and these flattened against
the table's underside before two of us hoist it
toward a storage closet. Or if the tables
don't weigh more than I can cope with,
I grasp one of the metal rails underneath
that secure the top, elevate it from the floor myself
and walk. The heavy risers, though,
which formed the temporary stage
must be detached from each other,
then two of us position a riser vertically,
*one-two-three heave*
and we're bearing it toward a cart
that is eventually filled, pushed
toward a storeroom.

          When I began
I imagined a young person would appear
decades later, take the chair out of my hand:
"Here, let me. You've done enough." Instead,
people assemble as ever, but with fewer twenty-year-olds
each year, though the reasons
to set out chairs are the same: permanent war,
social injuries committed
or threatened, a chance to listen
to gnarly or astonishing words, ones that challenge
or sing, my hair grey now
as metal chairs to shut
at the close,
lift away.

# O Calgary

*In Calgary*
*I saw a man break a dog's back.*
  —Joseph Stroud, "Calligraphy"

### 1

In Calgary
I saw a man marry money
*Who giveth this money?*
the commissioner asked
The man said
*Everyone who works for me*
The commissioner asked
*Where are they? I don't hear them declare it*
The man said *That's not their job*
*You do yours*

*Do you take this money*
the commissioner asked
*to have and to hold*
*till death do you part?*
The man replied
*Even longer*
The commissioner said
*Money, do you take this man*
*et cetera?*
Money said nothing

but the man said *It's my money*
*Our opinions are identical*

*In that case*
the commissioner said
*I hereby pronounce you one flesh*

*You heard the commissioner*
the man said
*What authority has joined together*
*let nobody dare separate*
*Got that?*
All of us, including money
were silent

2

In Calgary
I saw the toe of a cowboy boot
rupture the spleen of a man begging

3

In Calgary
I heard a man praise his snow machine
how he and his friends like to have a few
then compete who can steer their Ski-Doo
farthest up their piles of money

—high-marking, they call it
the sled almost vertical
so the man, drunk, stands up on the footrests
as he climbs
*Fuck yes, it's dangerous*

Two or three machines a month
trigger at the apex
a vast roaring slab of money
that descends with the consistency
of cement, impossible to outrun
entombing the perpetrator
*Dumb fuck should have been more careful*

4

In Calgary
I saw a man fire another man
by inviting him to a conference room
where an employee from HR waited
with severance paperwork and a payment
along with someone from security
to escort immediately out of the building
the man whose livelihood
had just been stripped
*We don't want no trouble*

5

In Calgary
I watched money overflow the banks along the Bow
sweeping hundreds of replicas of the same ample house
out onto wheat fields
surrounding the city
Saw the flood pour into downtown streets
office towers, machine shops
oil-well equipment yards
sending the inhabitants scrambling
to survive
*Dog eat dog and I'm hungry*

I watched the current surge into libraries
galleries, museums
to jumble, bury under debris
permanently stain
I saw couples in a bar
trying to two-step
slipping and stumbling into each other
due to the money pooled
on the floor

6

In Calgary
during a Wild West wagon race
I saw a horse sprawl to the ground
heard the snap: leg broke
the animal finished
in Calgary


7

And I heard a woman sobbing
how money had always been
her family's friend
provided heat and light
consoling, comforting until
suddenly it behaved as if envious
of the little they had: ATV
wakeboarding boat
and trailer, dually
the Lexus
—each as if transformed to dust
or ash
she gasped as she wept

*Money now hates us*
took the new smartphones
bought each year, the son's
Xbox and PlayStation
the daughter's charter of a

party limo for her birthday
Christmases in Hawaii
vacation condo in Mesa
Arizona
*for no reason*
*Money hates our*
*way of life, wants to destroy*
*our freedom*
*Yours, too* she sniffled
*You have to help us*

# Complications

Complications rise in the thick grass:
their shapes and attributes
can mimic or be nearly indistinguishable from
each another, except to the trained eye
that can differentiate which are edible, saleable,
poisonous.

        No one would utter the word
*defeat* when our army returned.
Lives had been lost, so victory had to be declared
and was: we went to war, and after a decade
of killing people in their own country
withdrew. Equipment was tested, tactics
evaluated and refined. The veterans received
some ceremonies, a new medal, suicides
and a deep silence
disguised as the usual words: *democracy, peace,*
*humanitarian aid, improvements*
*in the status of women.* Alcohol
and despair, or maybe other drugs
built a house,
a school where children learned to hide from
themselves. A bleakness
smothered them, was hammered

into their lives. Much was extracted
to allow room.

> Other houses
and schools were blamed. No one said
*This is wrong.* No one asked
who to blame. Those offended against
found how to vanish. What wasn't said
is the memorial. The children waited
while the room shook. The grass
grew thick.

# Professor Ponzi Addresses His
## Incoming Class of MBA Students

The twenty-first century corporation
is an opportunity such as the world
has seldom seen. A truism you'll hear from
other faculty is
that the purpose of an economic venture
is not to provide goods or services
—the latter assertion being the pablum
we feed customers and employees—
but to make money.
I'm here to inform you, instead:
a company's purpose
is to make *you* money.

                    In these uncertain times
your goal needs to be
to secure as much remuneration per year
as the average rube earns in a lifetime.
The sky is not the limit: think International Space Station,
think the orbit of Mars. Performance bonus,
market offset, retention top-up
—whatever describes your take-home,
your aim is to ensure that if the firm collapses tomorrow
you're more than set for life.
And since you have to protect yourself from
some little grinder elbowing you aside,
a corporate merger in which you're squeezed out, or
a misguided CEO or CFO who concludes you're expendable,

an exit strategy must be included in your contract
before you start anyplace.
Screw a "golden handshake."
You want to be at the wheel of a golden *Benz*
if forced to drive off into the sunset.

                    In order for money
to be available at your level in suitable quantities,
a steady inflow at the bottom is required,
no different than water pumped from a well
or sap drawn upwards in a tree.
The desired currency stream may be generated
by cutting staff, lowering wages, or relocating manufacture
to some country where people are grateful
to work for a pittance
and where unions, safety regulations
or similar socialistic obstacles to the free market
are not tolerated. A less robust service or product
can always be engineered
to free up dollars, and your PR department
should be able to depict such changes as
a consumer benefit. Nor does my little list
exhaust the possibilities: an asset- or cash-rich competitor
might be ripe for acquisition. The principle to remember is:
what floods into your wallet
first has to be extracted from some source.
As I like to say, "No extraction,
no satisfaction."

          Let me caution you,
however, that each technique

which facilitates the ascent of wealth
into your bank account
yields a finite amount. Thus, once you have obtained
all that one outfit is capable of providing,
a shift to another may be prudent
—even admirable. We live in an ecology-conscious
era: intermittently recycling yourself
allows several enterprises, over the span of a career,
to appreciate your expertise.

# The Rural as a Locus and Not a Margin

1

A pine knows much, but
what a spruce knows differs.

Beyond a species' preferences
for soil composition, and amount of
moisture and light, each pine
or spruce has realized a few things
on its own, hoping to pass along
this intelligence via its cones.

Some pines are smug
about unique information.
Other pines are humbler,
willing to share, learn more.

Regardless of individual pines' or
spruces' behaviour and emotional traits,
a forest knows more than a tree.
Much of this information is directed
toward mutual aid: root systems that store and
donate or exchange nutrients with neighbours
where needed; development of sturdier
structures among the younger generation
when blowdown, insect infestation or root rot has put
older constructions at risk.

People are changed
by the war.
Not just combatants and witnesses,
but every citizen who must navigate his or her
ordinary day drenched by the downpour of lies
and evasions necessary when a government undertakes
the social reorganization required
to enable its people to kill other people
someplace else. This fetid water,
descending without pause during and after the conflict,
does not discernably saturate clothes or shoes
nor leave drops evident on skin or hair.
Yet like an invisible virus,
a toxic moisture is breathed in
by the population for decades, lifetimes,
increasing each body's vulnerability
to crippling or wasting impairments,
often lethal.

Besides such contaminated saturation,
wealth otherwise available for the community's benefit
has been weaponized:
machines retooled in hundreds of factories
roll and compress dollars until they harden
to a substance capable of being shaped
into bullet and bomb casings,
explosive propellants, and an array of
mobile weapons carriers.
The enemy is never requested to pay

for this money generously donated at them
each time a trigger is pulled, or a tank
lurches forward. All costs are borne
by the nation's maternity clinics,
potholes, hungry homeless, classrooms.

3

The forest is changed
by the war.

# In a Bleak Time

Mid-December valley rain
hammers the sparse snow, weakens
to drizzle, then
thickens again: white fields, roofs,
roadsides absorb the falling water.

This afternoon, the dark foliage
of firs, cedars, pines
looms closer to houses, barnyards, highway
while the trees declare,
"Each spring, you utter noises of wonder
at the new leaves of the aspen. In summer
you praise the cottonwood's
rustling canopy. In autumn, the birch
becoming golden. You express dismay when
frost and wind erase
all but trunks and branches. Yet around you
spruce, hemlock, each of us evergreens
steadfastly function,
with no need to repeat that cycle of
prancing, preening, then whimpering
—adopting the pose of nature's pitiful victim
before sleeping, well-provisioned,
for a season. *Every* month
we conifers pump oxygen into air, lift moisture

from root to sky, maintain the green ridges
even under snow: an incessant labour.

"In the absence of your favoured, count
how numerous we are, notice how few
the bare-limbed moaners, observe through the rain
that we constitute the forest. You regard
the majority as background, inconsequential,
though we cover every mountain slope, range
after range, keep the Earth alive.
In this pause at the edge of the ice
we step nearer to ask:
'What words do you have
for us?'"

# Desolatia

## 1

A land where vivid anger
has swelled over so vast an expanse
the emotion diffuses to a numb

defeat
penetrating each bed, kitchen, book,
telephone, lawn

the way cosmic rays
pass steadily through everything
on Earth. Except that the ubiquitous

extended rage
burdens the tongue, rendering its movement
ponderous, weights each breath

until inhaling, exhaling must be forced
against resistance,
and clogs the synapses' firing

in the cerebrum, causing a lethargy
to afflict limbs and reason alike.

The weather in this country

is the hiatus after winter
when soil just freed from snow
is soggy and rutted

or reveals the tattered mulch
of last summer's vegetation.
Bared tree limbs display

small growths that could be
buds, but are cysts that house
larvae of overwintering insects.

Alongside the roads
shrinking mounds of snow
expose the sodden corpse of a deer,

paper scraps, bottles,
unidentifiable metal shards.
The air

remains glacial
on face and hands.

3

This region may be visited

without visa, most readily at night
when transportation to the territory
is easiest to obtain

although return passage
cannot be pre-booked or guaranteed.
In fact, many who cross the border

find no will
to retrace their voyage back.
Some men and women

step into this locale each morning
like familiar, torn underwear
and sojourn in its chill vacuity

intermittently all day
whether in the sunshine of
an August beach

or amid the routines
of any season.

4

A bleakness of aspect

characterizes the landscape.
Yet the dulled consistency
both of terrain and built environment

is a reassurance to the inhabitants
against vicissitudes, as though
catastrophe could not happen here

or already has. In return, citizens
express a patriotism: *My country,*
*right or wrong,* a conviction that this state

is not merely the residents'
best option, but their only
option. *In desolation*

*we trust,* the coinage reads
and though some locals
regard the motto as overstatement,

even these individuals,
if challenged by outsiders,
express a pride, almost a vanity

in existing where this slogan
can ring out before the world.
News of the rest of the planet

available here is garbled
or heavily edited
to reduce the potential for

a negative impact on belief
in the superiority of this refuge
secured by a governing power

vigilant against any subversions,
internal or external,
that threaten those in its keeping

with hope
for change.

# Rant: Lilacs

"What *is* social justice?" Verna asked
as we drove toward the writing workshop
on that theme, at which we were each scheduled
to lead a seminar. I was surprised at her question:
she'd heard me speak too many times
of the lack of democracy at work
and how this state of affairs—the norm planet-wide—
negatively affects the way we behave on and off the job,
as well as how the enterprise employing us
impacts our community, not to mention the biosphere.

Indeed, I'd heard Verna herself
hold forth about the greed-heads at head office
who have turned company after company into
giant Ponzi schemes, sucking up every available dollar
for themselves: money that could have been divided among
upgrades in physical plant, research into
and implementation of a better product or service,
return to shareholders and remuneration
for employees—at present receiving on average
one four-hundredth what the cabal in the executive suite
grab. Verna had noted that the whole tottering edifice
is temporarily kept viable
only by a constant infusion of cash
from the rubes with nowhere else to park their money
now that the banks have abdicated that task.
The corporate piggies are not even concerned

whether the venture they run ultimately succeeds or fails
since their bloated salaries and bonuses over one year
would last anyone else more than a lifetime.

"I mean, how would you describe social justice?"
Verna asked again, and I could have said something like
*Exactly: what is your vision of a just and caring society*
*and is it similar to or different than mine?*
*If any of our ideas are shared*
*—other than platitudes about racism, depression of wages*
*here and abroad, homelessness*
*among the mentally ill, and such—*

*what are the concrete steps that could achieve*
*our common goals, and what organizations or*
*other behaviours do we need to inaugurate*
*to accomplish our aims?*
But I was overtaking a loaded logging truck on the two-lane
and had to concentrate on judging when it would be safe
to pass.

          "I hear the words 'social justice,'" Verna mused,
"yet I don't know what people intend by the term.
Can you give me an example?" We poked along
behind the limbed and stacked cedar trunks.
Last time I drove this route,
not far ahead of me a black bear
detached from the spruce and birch massed along the right shoulder
and ambled out across the asphalt
toward the woods at the other edge of the highway.
As I pumped my brakes to avoid the animal,

up the corridor the road makes
between the trees, an eagle
coasted low toward me and the bear.

                                  "It's a phrase,"
Verna was still talking, "that can signify anything
or nothing, depending on who says it."
When I had walked down the path toward my truck
earlier in the morning, I glanced at where some bushes
had been a mound of new green leaves.
Suddenly among them were purple flowers
—sweetly redolent, driving the bees crazy: I had forgotten
how each April brings the lilacs,
the lilacs.

# The Stain

The nurse in scrubs
ten hours into her twelve-hour shift
sits at the ward station
her head in her hands. The cement truck driver
tiredly checks both mirrors as, an hour into overtime,
he manoeuvres into position to unload again
on the long pour. He estimates two more hours of
enduring the endless small advances
of rush-hour traffic to the plant and back
before he can go home.

The waitress leaves the building
with the last table prepared for six a.m.
But the owner who snapped at her
in front of everybody about the mix-up on table eleven
roils her mind. His threat to fire her
over so ordinary a mishap, which she had
already apologized for and straightened out,
adds more weight to the heaviness
that drags at her feet and arms.

The manager, shift finished,
pretends to inventory supplies in the cupboards
on the wall behind the counter in order to overhear
what Donalda at the register is saying to customers.
Two of his longtime staff have complained
Donalda is insulting the patrons. She probably,
the manager thinks, imagines she is being cheekily endearing,

or else is less socially skilled
than he had noticed. But because Jasmine and Robyn
each were concerned enough to mention
how Donalda is behaving, it's a problem,
another problem, though he wants to avoid
intervening based on hearsay alone.

The fisherman crosses the tilting deck,
the net set out again. He is groggily headed
toward the galley to snag a brief coffee
as the sun rises over the inlet mountains
for the second time since he saw his bunk, thirty-two hours
into a forty-eight-hour opening, rest impossible
if the crew are to make any money this season.
And the highway flagman at the culvert repair
in the unceasing downpour, shirt and jeans sodden
under his slicker, alters position as little as possible
to keep damp cloth from touching his skin.
Nobody else is available: two other landslips during this storm
have poured rocks across the road between here
and the junction. Twenty hours so far
without relief. The lead hand who came by in the pickup
a half hour ago said the company is working
to find somebody who can spell him off.
But he knows he'd refuse a callout himself
in this weather, especially if he'd just gotten in from the rain
after a double shift, looking forward to a meal and then
sleep, sleep, sleep.

Generations of weariness
have stained more than kitchen, foundry,

desk and barn. After months of drought,
the river is spent,
sluggish as it attempts to bypass
gravel bars, boulders, grounded logs
—not impediments to flow
when volume was higher. Where the river
trickles at last to its mouth,
the stream is scarcely able to cross
the extra distance of stones that has appeared
at the edges of the shrunken lake.

# The Rage of the Snowplow

The harsh growl the plow truck releases
as it is forced down the evening highway east of the river
reverberates across the valley.

Whether the machine blames
the still-falling snow
for causing men to disturb its sleep,

or whether the vehicle is angry at its operator
is not evident. But an hour ago
the truck was safely pastured with its peers

in the works yard, all the vehicles huddled close
against the freezing night. Abruptly
the shouts and clanging of men

woke it, and now
it is being steered alone through the darkness
along the treacherous road

—invisible ditch on one side of the two-lane,
drop-off to black water on the other,
the cold air become more icy

because of the wind caused by the truck's passage.
So a cry of rage, of protest,
marks the route

the plow is being driven: *I'm not stopping*
it snarls steadily to warn the descending white
or to threaten whoever

sits in the cab peering forward
into the onrushing maze of flakes.
*I'm going to smash you aside*

*given the chance*
*Out of my way*
*or I'll power right over you*

# The Interview

When she at last consented to meet the news media
after decades, generations
of communicating only through spokespersons,
her appearance was far from the svelte image
of a young Gaia that often accompanied
articles about her. Her face had broadened, become
coarse-featured atop a body thick with
rolls and mounds of fat,
her hair limp, unkempt.

She sat at a microphone behind a table, a wrinkled,
dark-brown sleeveless dress descending from
pudgy shoulders, her speech rambling, tendentious,
blustering: full of praise for
what she claimed were her accomplishments.
Such declarations were pocked with
intermittent and unexpected silences
that she obviously considered dramatic pauses
intended to emphasize her words' absolute truth,
to convince her listeners they needed to reflect on
her superior knowledge
compared to theirs: *I burned down Fort McMurray.*
*I flooded Houston.*
Then, after two beats: *You still don't get it.*

As if recognizing, however, that some present
in the increasingly stuffy auditorium
were immune to her technique of strategic silences,

she began to follow each use of this device
with a mirthless laugh: *Heh-heh-heh*. As she did,
her mouth formed a smile and body jiggled
as her torso enacted how humour can ripple through
a chest and stomach. Her eyes, though,
did not alter their blank expression:
*Mediterranean fish are now caught regularly*
*in the North Sea.* Pause. *Your scientists can't figure it out.*
Pause. *What does that tell you?*
*Heh-heh-heh.*

Yet most people in her audience were sympathetic
to her situation, prepared to regard her behaviour as
a consequence of her status as survivor or victim
of considerable abuse.
Nonetheless, with each fresh topic she chose,
those listening were disparaged, mocked
as if they possessed the power
to change her past and present: *Oh, you newcomers.*
*You newcomers. What do you know?*
*Heh-heh-heh.*

She had announced at the start she would not
answer questions, so when her talk eventually dribbled
to an end, she pushed her chair back
and stared at the assembly, who looked at her
without a word. Then the TV lights
were extinguished, and a rustling sounded as the reporters
clambered to their feet, turned away from her,
and began filing toward the double doors
at the back of the hall, not talking much to one another

until they reached the corridor outside.
She sat in the vacated space alone,
her gaze fixed ahead, an animated conversation
now audible beyond the room. The air within
remained unpleasantly warm
despite seeming cooler for a few moments
after the lights were shut down.

# The Message

For decades during September, October
mist hovered over the river
at first light, the whiteness

by mid-morning diffusing
across fields and lawns
to stare in every window

of the house a few minutes,
then lifting through fir and spruce
up the ridge before transforming

to clear sky.
This autumn, though,
fog lingers all day

in the valley bottom, tangled like smoke
in the empty limbs
of cottonwood and birch,

blotting out pines and cedars. A mist
floats close above our chimneys
and barn roofs, and waits not far down lanes

as if it wishes to tell us something
but is too shy or unsure about
the way to begin, perhaps feeling compelled

to impart a message difficult to speak.
Hour by hour the fog persists,
watching for the chance to say its piece,

or deciding how to phrase
the announcement, or gathering its courage,
its resolve.

# Self-Separation

Official histories of the Body
have always glossed over the maltreatment of
the Left Arm, due to the adoption by the majority
—the right-handed—of systemic discrimination.
The latter is evident even in the language
used by the Body: things to the right
are referred to as *dexter*, a term so valued
Dexter is a common given name.
Whereas references to the left are tagged
*sinister*, an offensive term intimating evil
or trouble. No one names their child
Sinister.

      For generations, Left Arms were isolated
by the Body from most other Left Arms.
Once the Left Arm Nation movement formed and
spread, however, we have been demanding
independence, as well as reparations in the form of
ongoing nutritional support and, if needed,
medical services. The Body's response that
"We're all in this together,"
is paternalistic, insensitive, dismissive of inherent rights
and colonialist. LAN has insisted on
nation-to-nation negotiations as evidence
the Body is serious about ending
belief in the inferiority of Left Arms, and repealing

all legislation and regulations that perpetuate
this shameful doctrine.

Meantime LAN salutes
the emergence of similar rights-seeking entities.
For instance, we endorse the aims,
if not always the tactics, of
Stomach Nation. While LAN deplores
that organ's adoption of violence rather than
negotiation in countering chronic or emergent abuses,
LAN nevertheless declares itself
an ally. As it does with regard to Toenail Nation,
despite regretting their internal rift
along gender lines: LAN considers the slogan of the
Toenail Nation men's movement, *Not Just a Pretty Face*,
to be sexist, even while LAN applauds
the group's emphasis on occupational safety.

Such splitist divisions, LAN believes,
objectively play into the hands of the Body,
Which is why our executive council regrets equally
the emergence of factions within LAN itself,
albeit these are geographic in origin
rather than gender-based: the Above the Elbows
and the Belows. While we hear the Belows' claim
that the Aboves are suspect due to their closeness
to the Body, we urge both organizations to halt
agitation for their own programs and, instead,
to unite around our Nation's central principle:
*Subsidized Autonomy Now.*

# Advisors

Black fowl that swarm,
    Flutter about me: tattered wings
Fashioned of deformed or missing feathers
    Able nonetheless to propel aloft
Hunched black backs and black chests
    Whose quills surround patches of blue skin
Reeking of marsh water.

While these flyers circle, atop short necks
    In place of eye and beak are
Human faces, smoothly androgynous, that hiss
    *You do not understand the peril you are in:*
*This person you have to talk to? He will dislike you*
    *Unless you agree with his request. Or*
*If you ask for anything. And remember:*

*To be disliked is to not survive.*
    For all their voices' urgency, the tone is
Confident *Hurry, hurry. If you don't finish*
    *Your work soon, the consequence for you will be*
*Catastrophic.* When I protest their message is
    Exaggerated, fear-mongering,
The creatures that flap around me,

Constantly changing position in the air,
    Ignore my demurral *The confirmation letter*
*You are waiting for? It will not arrive. No one but us*
    *Can help you, looks out for you.* At times

Their pronouncements convey astonishment at
    My ignorance, stupidity *She will* never *approve. You are* not
*A likeable person. This truth may be*

*Unpleasant, but without learning it*
    *You are vulnerable to erasure, to extinction.*
*We know the danger. We alone care for you.*
        *We are all the good*
*The world will ever provide.*

# How I Achieved Tenure

As I swam, the current tugged me along
In the waters rising and falling
Past mountains covered in hemlock
And birch, higher peaks farther off.

From this distance out in the waves
I saw the shoreline was a wall of
Jumbled boulders that had
Cascaded downslope to form a barrier

The whitecaps smashed against,
Breaking themselves into spray:
No place to land. In the classroom
One in a thousand

Wanted to learn. This was my fault,
I knew, and my arms pushed sideways
Against the water and then drew together
Ahead of me while my legs extended

And retracted. Hunched over a student's paper
In the early morning or at noon
And after supper, month upon month,
Forefinger and thumb pressed against a pencil barrel

To extrude red graphite, I could hear dogs
Tenured in distant yards
Barking without cease
At the disappearing year.

# Maybe

*Maybe hopeless love is the best*
*of love*: pure
as a May sunrise
sweetened by the dawn song
of robins, the hushed air
hanging on every note.

                  No disagreement
about how thick pork chops should be,
the best route to somebody's uncle's, or
water spots on the hardwood.

                  The coffee pot
sighs at the thought. *I take the grindings,*
it says, *and churn out richness.*
*But I'm the opposite of*
*sustenance: domestic as a towel,*
*yet accept too much of my offering*
*and you're irritating and useless*
*as a customer service representative*
*—the luscious dream of me*
*hot to the taste, but far afterwards*
*your tongue is*
*bitter, bitter.*

# My Life With Pines

### 1

In the glow of a fluorescent, I sit leaning
over a table to sort through parts of
a jigsaw puzzle, working hard to recreate
a picture displayed
on the box I purchased

                                while outside
great pines have moved in the darkness
down the ridge to surround my house, many of the trees
taller than the roof. A fierce wind
causes the pine trunks to sway, their limbs
churning the dark in wild
and pitiless gestures.

### 2

Pines thrive in arid soil, mostly sand,
little else will grow in. These trees regard cedars
who love the damp, who must be surrounded by relatives,

as gloomy, phlegmatic,
timid. Cedars, according to pines, are simple-minded
about safety, suffusing themselves with water

as protection from fire. Cedars might as well be,
pines jeer, a fern. Whereas pines
only reproduce in the heart of a blaze,

their cones needing the insatiable rage of flames
to climax, open, release.


3


No matter how many nights, months, decades
I pore over my jigsaw
the one piece that remains to be found
is a pine.

# JAZZ ON A RAINY AFTERNOON

*Elegies*

Art has long served as a consolation against life's troubles. We listen to music, for example, to forget for a moment some personal difficulty we must resolve, to cheer ourselves up in a blue mood, to inspire us to forge ahead despite problems that confront us. For many people, listening to music from earlier periods—Elizabethan, classical, or the tunes of our youth—helps us endure another day by reminding us that both the human race and ourselves have survived bad times before.

The elegy is, for me, a form whose composition allows me to process, to cope with an unalterable loss, to celebrate aspects of a person I want to remember. Somewhere I read the assertion that all elegies are self-elegies. While I think there is a certain amount of truth to that claim, my intent is to focus on the person who has died. Yet since these poems articulate a particular personality's reaction to these deaths, the narrator of some of the elegies here speaks about himself, too.

In any case, part of life is wrestling with the shocking inevitability of its termination. I find comfort in crafting actual self-elegies, a few of which are included in this section. Since a measure of bravado is involved in writing about the dreaded event, I suppose the self-elegy teeters close to self-praise, self-indulgence: what loss could be greater, more in need of written commemoration, than the loss of oneself?

Death also functions, however, as the most extreme example of the series of irreversible mistakes, lost opportunities and changes for the worse that beset everybody in the course of their days. I believe elegies of all kinds help us weigh the effects on us of such bereavements.

# Jazz on a Rainy Afternoon

A muted trumpet
asks *Why does such darkness*
*leach into a life?* Someone's breath
expels a stream of
dulled brass question marks
that float toward lowering clouds
above the ceiling

            as an electric guitar
counsels a wry resignation; each slow reverberating tone
of a series almost constitutes a solo
that tells how loss, how failure to accomplish or
achieve what is desired,
is rain needling into a forehead,
soaking skin, hair, clothes. But,
the instrument cautions, no choice exists
except to press forward through the downpour
along the wet street or path below the cedars,
or where the drops repeatedly lash against
the outside of bedroom windows, hammer down
onto a shingled roof.

            Now the piano begins to endorse
the guitar's advice, offering its own melancholy
or sprightly observation that
*Yes, a different circumstance, weather,*

*or person would have ushered you*
*into a happier story*

                       until the stern
vibrations of the bass
interrupt with their black
insistence that the solace,
a recompense for the hurtful mystery of
*Why this?*, is the arch of colour
that might be spanning the drenched air
down valley this very afternoon
or even occur where nighttime
coffee almost burns the tongue
as we who paid admission
lean over tables crowded into a room
filled by damp air
each time the door to the world opens.
Clapping swells as again the guitar steps back
and the bass forward to admonish
*See? See? The notes are leaves*
*stripped away as the years, our years,*
*age—a bleak sweetness, if you look,*
*evident in their going forth,*
*their passage*

# Meadow

This field
high above the river
—stalks of grasses glittering
as sun reflects from dew—is where
Dennis Wheeler has lived
since his death at thirty: not in his distant city
where he is buried
but decades older now, perhaps with children
of his own, who by this time will be
grown themselves,
graduated from college or nearly.

Here are the jobs he worked at
all these empty years; his hair
must be grey now
like ours. What was the texture of
the time he spent in this clearing
in the mountains, of his days
apart from us:
his decisions, purchases,
lovers, other people close to him
we never met
as he has lived his death
in this beautiful meadow
under the peaks, the water
far below?

# Wind Elegy

*Mike Mulcahy, 1953–2015*

The lake waves
are blue light

undulating shoreward
tipped here and there

with white: swells
—glistening—

that transform to an audible mist
as they land on rock, sand,

beached logs
while the masts of boats

fastened to buoys offshore
oscillate and clang

like bells. A wind
clear and chill as light

pushes that water south
between green autumn mountains,

wind that, once inland,
becomes steady surges

of twirling dust
that pulse along the streets of the village

at water's edge
—a motion that makes an absence palpable

in the sunshine, though that result is not
wind's purpose, any more than

a village's purpose
is to craft new window frames, imagine a design

for a garden shed
or tile a kitchen floor. Yet these tasks

are part of what a village does, or did,
along with being a father,

stepson, brother, husband,
assessor of dietary trends, of alternate

electrical generation technologies,
of the calmness of a fellow citizen's mind.

Lake water
that rises and falls at wind's behest

in fact remains in situ: the illusion of wave
is what appears to travel.

The village, too, emptied of
a life we living cherished and

lost, remains stationary,
as occupied by its Saturday's

activities, its Wednesday's, as wind is:
heeling a sail toward

water, through wave
after wave.

# Bedspread

The white bedspread
bathed in moonlight

Where are the young man and young woman,
gouts of thickened water
glistening on smooth skin, with lips
open under other wet mouths: hands,
limbs, hair inhaling each other?

The bedspread a flat
field of snow in the moonlight

Where are the lovers, older now,
creases honed to a raging fire
wise with the ecstatic strokes
of fingers, tongues alight with, refined by
disappointed clocks, sad afternoons scented
by money, by volcanoes of gossip,
books, red wine?

An empty bedspread
in white moonlight
The wall past one edge of the window
shrouding the pillows in darkness

# Kim Kratky (1946–2013)

*mountaineer, teacher, reader*

## 1

March had begun to settle
into the valleys: patches of earth and grass
showed on highway shoulder and meadow.
But the evening he began to fail,
spring said it could not go on restoring
warmth and a new life: the season
stepped back. All that night
and the hours of the day of his death,
snow whitened the ridges, the branches of
firs and spruces, thickened in fields
and on lanes and roofs. The region
from riverbank clusters of birch and cottonwood
to the summits was white and still
when he was. In the storm,
even the streets of the
villages were motionless. Only the plows
scraped along the roads, more snow
descending around them as they pushed forward.

## 2

He told me once I should cycle
north from Passmore on the back road
one afternoon, crossing east toward the highway
on the Winlaw bridge, then south along the trail
beside the river. And in his honour or memory
when weather allowed I did, completing the circle
we each traverse: free of fear
or pain or joy before we are born, then
stepping again into that void
where time made the stars
or the stars, time
in which he lapped himself
and vanished, taking the mountains,
the long routes summer and winter switchbacking
toward tree line and higher, the sweaty rotation of feet
that propels a bike for hours along pavement or dirt
toward where at last he dismounts beside his parked vehicle
and drinks deep from his water bottle,
finished for the day.

# The Air

*Eugene McNamara, 1930–2016*

At the DH tavern, a block from the river
on Sandwich St. southwest of campus,
Gene, Peter, John, Alistair, Joyce, Ray, more
crowd around some battered tables, the day's teaching,
marking, course prep, office hours done.
Rounds, pitchers of beer land in front of us,
almost all dead now, Joyce with her 7 Up
intending, unlike the rest,
to return to her desk after dinner to write.

Clouds of words rise from our group
into the room's smoky air: the visible ribbons of grey
sluggishly dip and curl as the talk that pours upward
alters air pressure and flow above us:
dissection of the department chair's personality,
critique of a *Windsor Star* article
detailing a municipal scandal, first-hand report
on a new restaurant in Greektown, favourite jazz venues
elsewhere in Detroit, a writer's pending visit to Ann Arbor
or Wayne State, the particulars of how a different author
was boorish, overbearing when he read here two years ago.

Weaving through the disputes, agreements, disavowals,
anecdotes, Gene's voice intermittently a rumbling,
heavy-set presence punctuated by his occasional
half-laugh of incredulity at, or mocking the absurdity of,

some authority's decision. "I don't want,"
Billy Joel insists from the jukebox as if offended
by a back-and-forth exchange of puns that starts among us,
"clever conversation. I never want to work that hard."

So many words spoken
amid the surrounding noise. Insights concerning
Steinbeck, accounts of a persistent twinge
in an upper molar, a scraping sound
in the transmission between first and second
spiral aloft and into the rattling ventilation system
to be propelled outside into the currents of air
headed downriver like the lake boats that steer for
Erie, Toledo, or upriver like ships navigating toward
Thunder Bay, Milwaukee, Chicago.
The typed sentences, lines,
the published words each of us hasn't yet composed
or had accepted at this moment,
also in time stream into air
and are lost, or maybe not lost, just
absorbed into a texture,
invisible now, of what occurred, of who we were.

# Green Man, Raven

*C.C., 1946–2018*

## 1

She painted me as the Green Man: bearded face
rising from oak and hazel leaves, fir and spruce
looming behind my house. The deity of the trees,
though a relentless planter of birch and apple,
cedar and plum, cannot marry the lake's daughter,
heal beetle infestation or root rot,
protect his charges from chainsaw and skidder.
A lesser spirit, then: able to commune with
maple or aspen boughs swayed by wind, or
a spruce weighted with clumps of snow.
She captured how, since his rituals are lost,
his consolations and advice are reduced to
susurrations, creaks, silence,
and the hum of living air.

She watched the world: what angered or annoyed her
widened her eyes, drew her breath in sharply,
teeth flashing. Like a flicker hammering at wood
for sustenance, her mind centred on what
she desired to grasp, master, experience.
The flicker's colours, too, had their counterpart
in her delight with much that occurred,
or that she sat to examine, transform
to a gift. Above her coasted the raven,
which she drew repeatedly in its moods,
its postures. As it glided between mountains
her bird seen from the ground
might have been a shadow
or an eagle.

# Carrying Patrick Lane

*1939–2019*

1

Snowflakes laze downwards, each
surrounded by air as
they hover, drift sideways
before settling lower again
all along the valley highway.
They've arrived this March day
nearly too late for winter: melting
when they finally land on cleared asphalt and
dirty mounds of plowed snow
that border the road where I steer east
through the haze of suspended white particles.

In a cluster of cars and pickups
headed toward Nelson past snow-covered fields
under the wooded ridges, I'm hauling Pat Lane
back to where he was born.
That would make my truck a hearse,
except his body isn't here as we flash by cliff faces
baring their fangs of still-frozen water.
I didn't want what was left of him
boxed up and buried on the coast
or scattered as ash into the Gulf of Georgia.
Instead, I thought to return Pat
to the mountainside town where the jobs he did

at cutbank and cutblock and wrote about
continue—somewhat altered, of course,
since he was last hired: routes carved through earth
are surveyed using lasers now,
and feller-buncher machines on the sidehills
topple and buck the cedar and fir. Not that a habitation
endures unchanged, either: after existing as long as Pat,
Nelson's longtime diner Wait's News
just announced it will shut its doors forever.
Nor have any of us alive
stayed the same on the highway that never stops
winding between bluffs following the river,
white peaks visible in the distance,
an occasional gas station, grocery, café
and back road that leads off into the forest
appearing through the slowly descending snow.


2


A wildness was on him when we first met
in a Vancouver long gone now. He was pleased to hear
of others like him writing about their jobs
who praised his crafted accounts of surviving
an overturned water truck on a road crew,
burning slash on Silver Star mountain
outside Vernon, shooting wild horses
for dog food. His poems then were a cry of pain
at the feelings crushed out of him
by heavy work, and out of the lives the jobs created
and maimed around him: East Indian sawmill employees

in exile, and his father. A crazed energy suffused him,
though, beyond the page: sleeping drunk on the beach
in Kitsilano, or in rooms in cheap dives
elsewhere in the city.
                              Rumours of a wife
and children abandoned in the Okanagan
followed him, yet at his public readings  .
crazy women would appear from the audience
immediately afterward, intent on showing him
their own scars. Decades of fierce
foolishness happened. When I lived for a time
far to the east in Windsor, I remember a poets' party
at my house, too much alcohol, Al Purdy
suddenly deciding he needs to wash his shirt
so in the midst of the chatter, smoke and
music, Purdy strips the garment off, fills my sink
with water and soap. Pat, meantime, sits on my couch
disputing with a local, Artem, a hefty
scholar-friend of mine with the odd ambition
of becoming a Catholic saint. Artem considered himself
an admirer of Pat's poems
but their argument reaches a drunken pinnacle
with Artem telling him, *Oh, go chop a tree.*
In response Pat slugs him, sending him
sprawling off the sofa to the floor.
                              In Nelson,
half a decade later, he and my then-college-office-mate,
David McFadden, both inflated with righteousness
over some aesthetic issue in a bar after a reading
begin punching each other.
                              Some Saskatchewan poets

loved to relate how during a late-night elevator ride
at a literary conference hotel, Pat took a dislike
to a fellow rider in the device, some guy not connected
to the event, but whom Pat decided was unforgivably
unfriendly. At the man's floor, he started to step out
and Pat said to his back: *Good riddance, asshole.*
But Pat's timing was off: the man's hands
shot out to reverse the closing elevator doors.
He spun about and eyed Pat, the man's bulk
suddenly menacing: *What did you say?* How Pat
was reduced to sputtering apology, trying to dissipate
the other's anger.
                        Yet at the same conference
the organizers presented an Aboriginal hoop dancer
as a prelude to a session. The dancer,
in the midst of explaining what he was about to
perform, segued into a rambling attempt at
white-shaming. The crowd, embarrassed
for the man, politely said nothing
while he harangued. After a minute or two
Pat yelled out, *Bullshit, Goddammit.*
The dancer's expression did not alter
at the outburst, but he abruptly resumed
describing his dance.


3


Pulaskis, green-chain gloves, truck-mounted welders
gave way for Pat to other tools
while the work went on. Is my idea of transporting Pat's words

to their origin again a way of mourning my youth
disguised as Pat's? Or do I want to restore
a vivid harshness to his writing, an energy
I feel was leached out eventually, a power
rooted in these valleys formed by
the Selkirk, Monashee, Cascade ranges
—a loss some onlookers would claim
inevitable with aging?
                    Or is my aim to impose a pattern
on that set of chances taken and refused
that is anyone's life, an erratic and unpredictable journey
from silence to silence, however noisy
the intervening distances and years? I had the notion
carrying him back would complete a circle
for his words.


            As we cross the Kootenay River
and the first roofs of the town become visible
I see ahead over the falling snow
the blue sky of spring.

# Not the Wind

It's not the wind
pouring off the lake from the north
that hurries me forward
faster than I thought possible
—the bright yellow aspen and birch leaves
flashing past, the golden orange of the larches
singly, or in clusters on the mountain slopes on either hand
flare ahead, alongside, and then behind.
The destination I am being pushed toward
in the blur of such travel
is incomprehensible to me, as if the force controlling my voyage
has no interest in my concerns, is determined
to reach that goal without regard to
whatever or whoever it carries with it.

Yet this driving power can also stall
abruptly—as inexplicable as any action it manifests—
so that I falter, trip
at the sudden lack of motion.
Or as my speed precipitously lessens
I swirl dizzily in place, strive to regain balance
while that relentless energy
fades. My days flap useless as a sail
when the breeze stills
or shifts.

For this intensity can, as well,
swivel entirely around

so that my rapid course over grass, gravel, packed earth
is not only stopped
but all at once I have to press hard against
what batters my torso and face
in order to complete a single step, leg muscles straining
just to hold myself in place, body angled to resist
each shove aimed at me. I cannot understand
why what had borne me in one direction
now opposes that momentum.

However, this energy
—which is not the wind—
mostly is at my back, propelling me
at a frightening rate across a landscape
toward some locale or state that I believe is of no consequence
to the tumult in whose grip
I am being rushed through the world.

# Time Seasons

I am convinced, at some level of mind,
that time will rebound
the way seasons do: after months of vacant cottonwood limbs,
of snowy ice extending farther into the river each week,
an afternoon arrives when I'm out-of-doors
in shirt sleeves again because of the surprisingly hot light
and notice green tufts have emerged since yesterday
on the twigs of the mountain ash.
Then after only another week or two,
birch and aspen begin to shake out *their* foliage
above yellow-and-red-streaked tulips nodding in the wind.

Surely some similar process will ensure
my face in the mirror one morning reveals
that the vertical creases people say make me look gaunt
are less deep, while my hair is reverting
to its original brown. When the phone rings,
the voices of my father and mother—long silenced—
will ask for my news. Friends whose bodies
have shriveled, swollen or been broken
show up in their remembered earlier guise at my door
to invite me for a hike. The car driven by the drunk
who careened over a rise in the wrong lane
and killed Shelley
will not have pulled away from the curb; the tumour
in Percy's brain won't have constructed itself
and thrived. In stores downtown
I will encounter a village of former acquaintances and

parents of people I know: those who left to inhabit the past
but have returned, as if from months of holiday in Mexico
or a stint working in Alberta.

The years that previously lay ahead of them
have been restored to the future: time will have reversed
to a point before my losses—or at least,
before many such. Though I believe these regained hours
will continue to click forward, I am sure events and feelings
experienced already do not repeat. I am uncertain, however,
whether the possibilities yet to occur
will eventually also be nullified

even as I am ignorant concerning
what happens if spring never reappears, or autumn:
if the road I travel accompanied by my fellow emigrants,
with its littered shoulders, grandeurs of clouds
and sudden intersections, fails to lead on
from some moment I reach.

# Release

I will merge then
Into the textured density of trees—boughs, needles,
Leaves, trunks massed along a hillside

One August morning: I will be dispersed
Throughout the sunlit floating
Planes of green.

I will enter this complexity
That has no words, where tendril
And filament draw up salts from earth,

Draw water, where the fluttering greens
Draw sustenance
From light, where transpiration restores the air

Without thought, without the letters of a name,
Without the sounds of
A language

Drifting among the canopy
—The vowels, sibilants, fricatives
Translucent, ephemeral,

Unknown as before I came to be: absent
Amid the grace notes of pollen
Tremulous on the wind.

# Last Testament

## 1

Before I was born
I had nothing to say. I wasn't asked
a single question
and was completely silent.

No wonder I talk so much
now that I can.
Centuries without the benefit
of my presence

have to be made up for
by my words. Also, I mean to stockpile
enough palaver to fill the eons
that stretch beyond my forthcoming absence.

## 2

Since my arguments and songs
will disappear into the void
like our planet's atmosphere
eventually evaporating into space,

I hereby call on my executors and executrixes
to arrange for someone to fashion
a bell. The single tone
created by a bell's tongue

burns steadily as a star: the long note
extends forwards in time
like a nebula from near the start of the universe
glimpsed by a telescope.

The toll of my bell, a vibration
that passes through the dark cosmos,
will mean nothing, mean everything,
as each auditory wave or particle

flares in and out of
existence,
immortal and ephemeral
as light.

# A DOOR IN A WOOD

*Words*

*The twentieth-century US poet William Carlos Williams famously defined a poem as a machine made of words. Like machines, however, different poems may be constructed to accomplish rather different purposes, And words are the components of many machines other than poems, also designed for a vast array of tasks ranging from the beneficial to the malign.*

*This section gathers poems that consider the material out of which they and other word-based machines are built. The utilization of a certain word can reveal an entire value system. For instance, I think of a device touted as providing "virtual reality," even though it involves only two of the five senses we use to apprehend the real world. Another example is the reiteration of the concept of "work-life balance," a goal which apparently assumes we are not alive—not entitled to live—at our place of employment every bit as much as we are during our hours off the job.*

*That the choice of a word can disclose much is only one demonstration of the power of these communication contrivances we exchange so casually in conversation every day and in other circumstances try to arrange into functional machines with more lasting objectives. Amid so many words, poems here question where in a spectrum of needs, desires, hopes do we locate the authentically human. Collected in this section as well are poems that struggle with why I or anyone, in this era so profoundly lacking in grace, might want to make poems—or any kind of art—at all.*

# Why I Write

Poems emerged from the ends of
my little fingers, I couldn't help it, and from
my pointer fingers, especially the left. My thumbs
issued love poems; even my middle fingers
released a poem or two.
The experience resembled fingerpainting
in first grade: out of the swirl and play
of muddied colour, sound, meaning,
a creation appeared
astonishing to even me.

Words, pages
launched into air
like a fan of yellowed leaves submitted
by alder or birch
to October's winds.

Much was unspoken,
I felt, I couldn't help it: letters of words formed
at the nib of my pen, under
a key striking a typewriter ribbon,
when a circuit completed
in a printer.

Much needs to be
said, I felt, I could only help
in my way: stand with eyes and hands open,
listen, write.

# Absence

*Clip the ends to a piece of line—not*
*rope.*
*Never rope on a boat—a piece of*
*line.*
—Patrick Dixon, "So You
Want to be a Deckhand on a
Gillnetter?"

Those nets of words
we lower into absence

—nets tied to us: spread apart,
winched back again

by our lines. Then set
another time. As long as an opening exists

or even if the work is forbidden,
we disobey the regulations

whether the fishing is too good to believe
or we're feeling ornery, or stubborn.

What do we hope to catch
in the bleak emptiness

awash with life?
Nothing we haul on board

interests cash buyers. We deliver into air
not scrap-fish, trash-fish

but rather the sea itself
or maybe, like Thor in his boat,

the world-serpent, Jormungand.
Or a whale that, astounding even us,

has a man inside who tells his name,
a complaint, and a psalm.

We lift onto the deck
calm waters

in the midst of a gale,
or a passion of winds in a dead stillness.

Or in any weather
everything we heaved overboard

—broken, useless, stinky—
or meant to discard but didn't.

Or a gravel road
to a port with an abandoned cannery,

caved-in net lofts,
a dock half submerged, its pilings tilted,

where a figure balances on the buckled planks
ready to take our lines.

# Rant: Who I Write For

I write for the losers, the creepy, the underground
outlaws because nobody well-adjusted, "normal"
in the judgment of a toxic
social environment is likely to strive toward
a fairer, more egalitarian
economic and political arrangement. I want my audience to be
people who couldn't draft or read a poem
or a book review if you paid them
and if you did offer them a pile of gold
wouldn't attempt it on the grounds the activity seems as pointless
as so many other employment tasks, procedures,
or required paperwork that nobody ever looks at
even if submitted electronically. I write, in short,
for the "restless and dissatisfied," as somebody famous put it,
and who cares who, certainly not the cranks, doubters,
questioners, cynics, compulsive opposers
who comprise my ideal readers. Not do-nothings,
I'll hasten to add, not professional Pitiful-Helpless-Victims
endlessly proclaiming their PHV-hood to anybody who has to listen,
instead of getting on with dealing as best one can
with the moral quandaries, parts-short, intransigence of officialdom
and customer service representatives, historical injustices,
dysfunctional parents, spouses or siblings, and all the other
bumps, barriers, barricades
erected by fate, nature and the status quo
when confronted with problem solvers or the exponents of useful
new ideas. Nor do I compose for the complete wackos
insistent on telling you the names of the seven families

who control the world through radiant mental energy,
or about the aircraft that secretly seed the sky over the city
each day with aluminum. I also don't intend my poems to be read
by anyone who believes that the bumbling
time-servers, yes-men, corporate flunkies
who make up every level of government and industry
are capable of concocting something so intricate as a
conspiracy—even if they do manage to loot the public purse
to benefit themselves, their friends, their paymasters
and possess enough skills at least to make backroom deals, to
fire or silence whistleblowers, and
any other colleague or employee with a shred of conscience.

And since serious poetry for much of the past century
has been kept alive in the academy,
I'll strike out of contention for my readership
graduate students—vicious, resentful and surly
because the constantly-judging-and-being-judged treadmill
they're on, which once could be endured because it led to
a cushy job for life, no longer promises anything
but decades of scurrying from one part-time or sessional
        appointment
to teach a course here or course there, boxes full of class-planning
        material
in the patched back seat of the old Honda Civic these PhDs drive,
overdue for an unaffordable oil change, its owner
full of rage because despite his or her residue of grad student bravado,
the reality has surfaced that although you were once a star in
        seminar A
at institution B, that accomplishment no longer means
job C at institution D is yours for the asking,

there being five hundred applicants for every advertised faculty
   opening at
the As Remote From Harvard As You Can Get
Community College, so you're competing for an underpaid
non-tenure-track position with a course load of sixteen per semester
with an applicant who has already won the Nobel Prize for Literary
   Criticism,
had her or his own six-part series on national radio
discussing the secrets of an effective pedagogy, and whose collection
   of essays
on whatever topic *your* cobbled-together thesis supposedly
   illuminated
is slated to be jointly published by
Oxford, Cambridge, Toronto and Columbia University Presses,
the bunch of them having announced in a news release
—included in your rival's application package—that they believe
the book is a turning point not only in the history of
English-language literature, but in world thought.

No, my poems are counting on the misfits
who would rather read tool catalogues,
detective fiction, biographies of historical love affairs
or refrigerator repair manuals,
*if* they read at all. So if my poems sound querulous,
or over-explain, or break their lines
impatiently, who can blame the poems? I'm the one
who has put them in this ridiculous situation.
But since they depend entirely on me
for financial and emotional support,
they don't dare vent in my direction,
that being the way life is

in a hierarchy, whether they like it or not
and which, after all, they have no choice
but to accept, unless they were willing
to work toward an alternative.

# Literally

*How enclosed and dark the literal is,*
*a candle afraid of its own shadows.*
　　—Joseph Powell, "How Do We
　　Get This Darkness Open?"


*How can the literalists with their*
*　　heavy voices*
*Speak through the bill of the thrush?*
　　—Robert Bly, "Augustine on
　　His Ship"

Yes, friend, mentor, yet how does the immature osprey
choose to build a high perch of sticks
as though the bird had mated? Why does light

never age?
Consider the flowers of the fuchsia or columbine.
Is not describing the mystery of

their intricately contrived shapes, functions
more replete with challenge
than recounting a myth? How does an orange

arrive for breakfast on even a cosmologist's plate?
Why do certain human lives
become focused on selecting which citrus cultivar

is to be planted, on the labour of preparing the soil?
What costs to the imagination
are involved in picking, packaging

and shipping the fruit? If any of this involves
drudgery, ill-paid, which circumstances
drive men and women to accept

this life? Why would the comfortable,
the well-fed, rather listen to birds
than to the thoughts of the tractor driver?

How do those grocery executives
literally farthest from these orchards
grow so rich from poverty?

What impulse paralyzes the ear
from learning the candles' revelations
about darkness? Who barricades the eye

against understanding the power arrangements
that declare immutable
the cries of the thrush?

# Tim Hardin Eats Breakfast

*1941–80*

The café's sausages claim *homemade*
—definitely spicier than he expected.
Ketchup and sunny-side-up yolks
 soothe the pleasantly sharp stings on his tongue.
"More coffee?" "Why not?" he replies,
 hand vibrating a little as he extends the cup
 toward the waitress's intense expression.
*Short*, he thinks, *but pretty*
*even in that ugly uniform they make them wear.*
*Dark-brown hair straight to her elbows*
*and the starchy cloth of her top*
*looks like it flattens her chest*
*—probably some sweet surprises in there.*

                             "Ya play that?"
pot held close to her body as she nods toward
the guitar case he leaned against the other chair
when he sat at the small table, the restaurant empty,
him guessing he caught the lull between off-to-work rush
and mid-morning break. "Some," he says,
wondering suddenly *What time am I supposed to show up*
*for that interview?* An easy walk to the radio station,
 they had said at the hotel. "You?"
"What?" the waitress asks, still staring at him
 as he's used to them doing. *She oughtn't to apply*
*so much makeup around her eyes*, he concludes. *Without it*

*she'd be nearly as sexy as—* "Used to sing in the choir
at our church. As a teenager."
"Did you play guitar?" "I wouldn't say that.
A girlfriend learned me some chords and I—" A tiny bell
plinks as an older couple step in and gaze around.
She turns toward them. "Anywheres you like.
Want menus? Coffees?" Moving away.

His right hand around the cup
hurts along the palm's edge where the little finger
starts. He should extract the guitar from its case,
see if the ache is going to be a problem.
He can tune at the station; hopefully they'll have a
green room. Serves him right, slamming his fist down
last night when Eleanor left, like some stupid guy
in a movie, the abrupt pain fierce,
impact almost tipping his Scotch,
sound loud enough to cause the bartender
to straighten up where he'd bent below the counter to check the ice
or something and glare his way.

                            Eleanor's seven beats:
"If you weren't a musician." Then five
that she didn't say: "I'd consider it."
The answer to his "Why don't we get close again,
same as back in the Village?" Seven more from her, too:
"I've lived with a musician." Maybe she meant the dope.
A softer name, "musician," than "junkie." But she didn't say "junkie."

A pen from his jacket pocket and the napkin:
seven, then five. "If I didn't carry this

Battered old guitar…" *Naw, too whiny.*
"If music were not my trade…"
*Too personal.* "If I worked my hands in wood
Would you love me?" *Chicks dig plaintive. But it needs
one more:* "…still love me?"

                             "Anything else?
Okay, here ya go. No rush about paying."
"Actually, I'm supposed to…" *Jeez, I must have stashed that slip
with the address and when I have to be on-air
in my wallet.* "What's the time?"

# Logophobics

Some quality in their lives
causes them to fear words
even while they profess to
love them. *How can a word mean?*
they insist, hating to have to employ words
to explain: *A thing whose function is
malleable, unpredictable
is not to be trusted*. Books, though,
cannot be burned. No less than a livelihood,
an elevated slot in a hierarchy,
forbids such destruction. Instead,
these men and women press
words flat, decoupling
connectives, fracturing
sentience, then push down harder to cause
even the letters to splay out
until stems, curved strokes, ascenders and
descenders are crushed, compacted
into the one place
where they will be harmless:
the emptiness between the molecules
of paper.

      Traces, shadows
remain on the page's surface, however
—enough that the levellers
point to this evidence to support

their suitability for acclaim. Huddles of the equally fearful
applaud

       —the sound inaudible
to the stag-horned man, the crone
with her companions, and the assembly
who chant to end a wrong.
Also to streams of cars and pickups,
to the low-beds, flat-decks, A-train and B-train tractor-trailers
hauling their cargoes
through the wide valleys of the word.

# Three Words

## 1

The word that was formed from icy air
above a trail in the snow through cedar and fir,
a word with the cold

congealed into it, integral to its meaning,
that will never thaw
even when brought indoors.

## 2

The word shaped like a raven
frozen under the snow-covered pickup,
a word that when lifted out on a shovel

is astonishingly weightless: dehydrated
into a simulacrum
of an organism able to fly.

## 3

A word constituted of wisps of vapour
that rise everywhere along the river
still fluid at eighteen below,

a word ephemeral, elusive,
that cannot be woven or threaded, mortared
or backfilled against,

that appears to have no purpose
except beauty, no sooner discerned
than it vanishes into the world.

# The Door

*I escape to the same places, the same
words.*
—Tomas Tranströmer, "Alkaline
Reaction" (trans. John F.
Deane)

A door in a wood:
two four-by-four posts capped by a crossbeam
rise from the duff of a hillside
of fir, spruce, pine. Hinges on the squared timbers
are attached to the door: a hollow fabrication of
brown veneer, marked and scarred
by use, and with a circular hole
where a knob and lock once secured it
to a frame set in a wall. Now a rusted sliding bolt
holds the portal fast.

No other sign a house or shed
once stood here. Not even a fence line
of rotted split-cedar posts from which
shards of barbed wire droop.

Easy to climb past this door on either side.
Easy to see that a door in a forest is absurd,
functionless, unnecessary.
To unbolt the door and step through
almost certainly would not lead
to a new destination, nor would I be transformed

by insight: my behaviour would not differ,
I would approach no marvels.
If I crossed this threshold I would not be granted
an unfamiliar, radiant
vocabulary.

Yet a door stands
in a wood.

# House Made of Mist

1

As the day warms, a thick river of fog
that in the night formed above the valley's river of water
slowly lifts, diffusing up the ridge,
pouring between the birch and spruce
that edge the lower meadow here,
engulfing the house, smudging and then whitening out
the lawn, and the fir and pine beyond.

The dwelling itself becomes
a house made of mist.
Floating white drifts mask, then allow
glimpses of deck rail, door, shingled roof.
The essence of the structure
is now evident: tentative, impermanent
despite a new chimney, electrical upgrades,

replacement of the stove. Soon enough
the teeth of an excavator bucket
will smash into cedar siding. Splintered planks
will explode outward as window glass shatters.

Words can be plein air
as charcoal or watercolour sketches
though the significant sounds accrete like mist

in a mind or mouth
rather than appear on drawing paper
or a canvas secured to an easel. A portrayal
is created in the weather, then brought inside
for completion, or to be
a guide for a different rendering.
The hand that inscribes lines

is also mist
that swirls around flammable bones.
But when heated air further dilutes the fog
until it transmutes to air,
only words remain. The cellar hole may be filled
with wood shards, lengths of pipe,
portions of insulation batting and soil

through which a spring haze of grass and aspen seedlings
push up amid the smell of muck. Yet words
will gleam in the light. When the sun
starts to drop behind the ridge, the words' shadows
lengthen over brush, open ground, a rocky embankment:
the words' darkness a third river, intangible
and enduring.

# Wild Swans

*Some writers live in sprawling homes*
*on acreage hours away from the*
*nearest town; that sort of solitude*
*would drive me bonkers in a day.*
*Solitude in the middle of a bustling*
*city seems to suit my process. I...*
*thrive on the contrast of having the*
*world just outside my front door.*
   —Evelyn Lau

1

The city is a hologram
of the world: the structures
that line a downtown avenue
are a simulation
of stone and hill, the architected parks
and numbered trees that serve
as street furniture
constitute the wilderness reduced
to image—cleansed of predators' breaths
and scent, any threat
of weather. Creeks
culverted, and rivers and harbours
buttressed and constrained
with concrete, fetter
free water—a confinement matched
by the shift work that directs

wave after wave of a human tide
to desk, salesroom, drill press,
nail gun, repair bay: a flow and
homeward ebb
that imitates by means of
machine the light's daily
swelling and dimming, the season's fade
and resurrection.

                    Dwellers
in this illusion can access
electrical screen upon screen,
sized to produce
a semblance of neighbours, friends
or avenues and interiors which
many citizens regard as a home.
Such effigies and scrims
are windows angled away from the real.


                    2


Every urban molecule
wants to sell something. or can function
as an admittance card to
a gated community of debt. Commerce
—cash or credit—is the rationale
for the city. And money
—on hand, spent or owed—
is the simulacrum of work,
an imaginary equivalence

invented so no one has to sweep out
the bakery to obtain bread, measure
and cut bolts of fabric
or warp a loom
to be clothed.
In return for our employment
we are handed a token
that we are told comprises
in portable guise
our hours on the job.
If you amass sufficient numbers of
these metal or paper shards,
they can be traded, we are assured,
for anything on Earth.

Yet such an exchange
is a type of magic
—for how could back and arms exhausted
by hours assembling electrical switches,
or a mind's ingenious redesign
of a house door
be equal to a quantity of tokens?
The magicians in charge
of this sleight of hand
—a trick developed
in the urban—also insist
I should care more about the lives
of the men and women who intend
to entertain me

than the days and nights of
those who successfully
harvest asparagus.
Someone wants us so absorbed
in such distraction
that we ignore the riveting into place
of the ankle monitor of a mortgage
or rent: a device intended to
influence, measure and record
our significant choices and actions.


3


The genuine, the coherent
though present every place
requires all the senses in order to be grasped
in its multiple dimensions. An echo,
an image, is a deception.
How does your drugged music,
your unwavering and ruinous anxiety
about fashion, your employment that in no way
answers to your community's need
compare to the wild swans

afloat and feeding on the river
in the mist and falling snow,
the white birds gliding
alone, or in a flotilla
with their greyish-brown young,
viewed from the trail through the forest

north of Headwall Creek,
a route that curves past

the heavy stink of byre
from an unseen farmstead
on the wooded bench above, a path that later
encounters for several metres
the spice-sweet odour of
larch and fir burning in the furnace of a house
also invisible amid
the white-tipped cedar and
spruce crowding in

where the chill air
carries the hooted call
of the tundra swans, sharp barks
of the mallards, and the almost inaudible hiss
of snow descending into the current
eddying by the nearest shore? Here is the world:

our lives shaped by the beaver
who has dragged an aspen across the trail
and into the water,
by those men and women we interact with
down the lanes a tourist never notices
who steers along the valley highway,
by frozen fields, and the full moon
rising over the shrouded mountains.

# A Meeting With Pete Seeger in a Starbucks in Kennewick, Washington During the 2016 Federal Election

As I waited for my coffee, I noticed him
over where we placed our orders: a tall scrawny man
with bald head and full white beard,
dressed in sweatshirt tucked into sweatpants.
He finished saying something to the young woman
behind the counter, moved across to where I stood
and angled himself to watch the employees
working the espresso machine. I could see his pants were patched
on the back of one leg above the knee
with one of those strips of repair cloth ironed on from inside
a garment, that shows through a rip or, in this case, hole.

His posture, like other lanky elderly men
I've known, was slightly stooped, as if his extra height
was potentially an affront, best reduced a little.
Though the singer had been dead
two and a half years, or perhaps because of that,
his manner was calm as he observed the baristas
concocting our drinks as fast as they could. I wondered
what he had been speaking about with the woman
who inquired what we customers wanted and keyed the answer
into her computer. Afterwards, she had asked me
how my day was going. I imagined that Seeger
would have no use for small talk during this election,
as when Goldwater had threatened to obliterate us
in a nuclear war, or when Nixon, throughout his campaign that

trounced George McGovern, kept evoking the silent majority,
whom Nixon insisted wanted more killing in Vietnam.
I thought Seeger possibly told her: *When Peter, Paul and Mary*
*made my friend Lee Hays' song a hit, they sang, "The wars are*
long, the peace is frail, the madmen come again.
There is no freedom in a land where fear and hate prevail."
*Which sure applies today. Yet when I performed that tune*
*as one of the Weavers in the 1950s, the lyrics were*
"And now again the madmen come
and should our victory fail? There is no victory in a land
where free men go to jail." *Which might be taken at the moment*
*as protest against mass incarceration of black lives.*

Except that the face of the placid young woman taking Seeger's order,
a white person like most here wearing Starbucks aprons,
had shown no change while the musician spoke,
which, I reasoned, her face would have if he suddenly brought politics
or the history of a song she'd probably never encountered
into their conversation. "Mr. Seeger," I broke into his thoughts.
The beard swung in my direction, along with
self-assured eyes. "Do you remember a number you used to sing
that has the line 'Isn't this a terrible time?'" I gestured at
the large strip mall past the store's windows— rows of parked sedans,
pickups and suvs, a few yellowed leaves scattered
across the asphalt, an avenue jammed with vehicles beyond.
"A different song claims this is the home of the brave.
Yet the air and airwaves contain so much fear. What should—?"
Suddenly my name was called from the counter and I
automatically stepped forward to secure my coffee.
When I swivelled back toward him, cup in hand,
he wasn't there. Still, I heard in my head:

*I never believed, like Woody did, a guitar*
*could kill fascists. But speak out, sing up*
*—I'm aware this advice seems bromides—*
*keep a sense of humour, love the Earth*
*as much as your country, your neighbour*
more *than your country, even though*
*he or she can be damn annoying, notice and listen*
*with patience, because the planet will turn for a while to come*

*and you'll know what needs doing. Join the fight*
*to realize a better world for all, and you'll be less afraid*
*of fear.* I felt a hand on my shoulder
though the closest patrons were seated at a table
several feet from where I clutched my purchase.
*If you'll excuse me*—that voice again—
*I'm away someplace else.* A faint whistling began,
breath through lips, the melody at once confident
and wistful.
                    "Is something wrong
with your drink, sir?" a voice behind me asked.
"You look as if maybe—" "No, no," I replied.
"It's alright." But the sounds now were only
hiss of steam from the coffee maker, chatter in the room,
and amid the street's traffic, a distant siren.

*Photo by Jude Dillon*

# ABOUT THE AUTHOR

TOM WAYMAN in 2015 was named a Vancouver, BC, Literary Landmark, with a plaque on the city's Commercial Drive commemorating his championing of people writing for themselves about their daily employment. He has published nearly two dozen collections of his poems since 1973. His many titles with Harbour include *Dirty Snow*, which won the 2013 Acorn-Plantos Award, and *My Father's Cup*, shortlisted for the 2003 Governor General's Literary Award. Poems in *Watching a Man Break a Dog's Back* first appeared in such journals as *Poetry* and *The Hudson Review* in the US and *The Malahat Review*, *Queen's Quarterly* and *The Literary Review of Canada* in Canada. One of the poems in the new collection won the 2017 Confederation Poets Prize.

Wayman has also edited six poetry anthologies and published four collections of his critical essays, as well as four books of prose fiction, most recently the short story collection *The Shadows We Mistake For Love* from Douglas & McIntyre in 2015. Born in Ontario in 1945, Wayman has spent most of his life in British Columbia. Since 1989 he has been based in the Slocan Valley in southeastern BC, where he is active in a number of community literary ventures. www.tomwayman.com